Junior High Bible Study Series

My Life as a Christian

Loveland, Colorado

Group's R.E.A.L. Guarantee to you:

This Group resource incorporates our R.E.A.L. approach to ministry—one that encourages long-term retention and life transformation. It's ministry that's:

Relational
  Because learner-to-learner interaction enhances learning and builds Christian friendships.

Experiential
  Because what learners experience through discussion and action sticks with them up to 9 times longer than what they simply hear or read.

Applicable
  Because the aim of Christian education is to equip learners to be both hearers and doers of God's Word.

Learner-based
  Because learners understand and retain more when the learning process takes into consideration how they learn best.

My Life as a Christian

Junior High Bible Study Series

Copyright © 2003 Group Publishing, Inc.

All rights reserved. No part of this book may be reproduced in any manner whatsoever without prior written permission from the publisher, except where noted in the text and in the case of brief quotations embodied in critical articles and reviews. For information, write Permissions, Group Publishing, Inc., Dept. PD, P.O. Box 481, Loveland, CO 80539.

Visit our Web site: **www.grouppublishing.com**

Credits
Authors: Keith Drury, Lisa A. Hitaffer, Siv M. Ricketts, and Amy Simpson
Editor: Kelli B. Trujillo
Creative Development Editor: Amy Simpson
Chief Creative Officer: Joani Schultz
Copy Editor: Loma Huh
Art Director: Sharon Anderson
Print Production Artist: Joyce Douglas
Cover Art Director/Designer: Jeff A. Storm
Cover Photographer: Daniel Treat
Illustrator: Matt Wood
Production Manager: DeAnne Lear

Unless otherwise noted, Scripture taken from the HOLY BIBLE, NEW INTERNATIONAL VERSION ®. Copyright © 1973, 1978, 1984 by International Bible Society. Used by permission of Zondervan Publishing House. All rights reserved.

ISBN 0-7644-2472-6
10 9 8 7 6 5 4 3 2 1   12 11 10 09 08 07 06 05 04 03

Printed in the United States of America.

Table of Contents

4 • Introduction

7 • Study 1: Rock Solid Faith
  The Point: You can trust God.
  Scripture Source: Leviticus 11:45   Judges 6:11-24, 33-40; 7:1-22
  2 Samuel 22:3   Proverbs 3:5-6
  Acts 17:24-25   Hebrews 11:11
  1 John 4:7-10

17 • Study 2: Guided by God
  The Point: The Holy Spirit lives within you.
  Scripture Source: John 14:15-17   Romans 8:9-11
  1 Corinthians 2:10-16
  Galatians 3:1-5   Titus 3:4-7

25 • Study 3: Everyday Grace
  The Point: We need to rely on God's grace every day.
  Scripture Source: Genesis 1:26-31; 3:1-24
  Exodus 20:1-17   Psalm 139:13-16
  Isaiah 55:8-9   Matthew 22:34-40
  John 3:14-21   Romans 3:10-18, 23; 6:22-23; 8:1-6
  Ephesians 2:8   James 2:10

37 • Study 4: No Matter the Cost
  The Point: Following Jesus involves suffering for your faith.
  Scripture Source: Matthew 5:10-12   Acts 6:8-15; 7:54-8:3
  2 Corinthians 11:23-29   2 Timothy 2:3

46 • Changed 4 Life

My Life as a Christian

Brenna was raised in church. She learned Bible stories in Sunday school as a little girl. She went to vacation Bible school every summer. She can't remember a time in her life when she didn't consider herself a Christian. She generally lives life by the book and, as usual, things seem to be going well for her. But sometimes at church, when she hears others talk about their close relationship with God, she can't help wondering if she's missing something.

Jackson made a faith commitment to Christ last summer at camp. Since then, he has started coming to church and has gotten involved in a youth group. He's trying to grow, but feels frustrated by some old bad habits he's unable to break. He considers himself a Christian, but often feels unsure if he's doing things quite right.

Joaquín was pretty pumped up about his faith when the school year started. He had recently renewed his commitment to Jesus and was determined to let it show in his life. So he started talking more openly about Christ with his friends. He even quoted a few of his favorite Bible verses. That didn't go over so well. In no time at all, he had earned the nickname "the preacher" and became the butt of jokes for weeks. So he began to keep his mouth shut. His excitement dwindled and he felt a bit betrayed. Nobody had warned him that his faith in Christ could cause him so much personal pain.

Brenna, Jackson, and Joaquín are all at different places in their spiritual lives, but they're all essentially asking the same question: "What does it really mean to be a follower of Christ?" In *My Life as a Christian*, you'll discover four Bible studies that will answer this essential question and will help students understand what it really means to follow Jesus.

In the first study, teenagers will learn what it means to make faith in God a central part of their daily lives. They'll discover that they can trust God completely and will be challenged to trust him even more.

Next your students will explore what the Bible says about the Holy Spirit. They'll find out that, as Christians, the Holy Spirit lives inside them and can serve as their guide through all of the difficult choices and challenging situations they face.

In the third study, teenagers will uncover what God's grace really means in their lives. Students will learn that they need to rely on God's grace every single day as they deal with their own sinfulness and their need for a savior.

The last study will help students understand that following Christ inevitably involves facing persecution for their beliefs. They'll be encouraged by biblical examples and will learn that even though following Jesus involves personal suffering, it is well worth the cost.

When your teenagers understand what it really means to be a follower of Jesus, they'll be prepared to weather the storms of life with their anchor solidly in place.

> **When your teenagers understand what it really means to be a follower of Jesus, they'll be prepared to weather the storms of life with their anchor solidly in place.**

junior high bible study series

About Faith 4 Life

Use Faith 4 Life studies to show your teenagers how the Bible is relevant to their lives. Help them see that God can invade every area of their lives and change them in ways they can only imagine. Encourage your students to go deeper into faith—faith that will sustain them for life! Faith 4 Life forever!

Faith 4 Life: Junior High Bible Study Series helps young teenagers take a Bible-based approach to faith and life issues. Each book in the series contains these important elements:

■ **Life application of Bible truth**—Faith 4 Life studies help teenagers understand what the Bible says and then apply that truth to their lives.

■ **A relevant topic**—Each Faith 4 Life book focuses on one main topic, with four studies to give your students a thorough understanding of how the Bible relates to that topic. These topics were chosen by youth leaders as the ones most relevant for junior high–age students.

■ **One point**—Each study makes one point, centering on that one theme to make sure students really understand the important truth it conveys. This point is stated upfront and throughout the study.

■ **Simplicity**—The studies are easy to use. Each contains a "Before the Study" box that outlines any advance preparation required. Each study also contains a "Study at a Glance" chart so that you can quickly and easily see what supplies you'll need and what each study will involve.

■ **Action and interaction**—Each study relies on experiential learning to help students learn what God's Word has to say. Teenagers discuss and debrief their experiences in large groups, small groups, and individual reflection.

■ **Reproducible handouts**—Faith 4 Life books include reproducible handouts for students. No need for student books!

■ **Tips, tips, and more tips**—Faith 4 Life studies are full of "FYI" tips for the teacher, providing extra ideas, insights into young people, and hints for making the studies go smoothly.

■ **Flexibility**—Faith 4 Life studies include optional activities and bonus activities. Use a study as it's written, or use these options to create the study that works best for your group.

■ **Follow-up ideas**—At the end of each book, you'll find a section called "Changed 4 Life." This section provides ideas for following up with your students to make sure the Bible truths stick with them.

Rock Solid Faith

"How can I trust God if I can't trust the people I know?"

Divorce, neglect, abuse, loneliness, adult responsibility, little to no opportunity. Today's junior high teenagers have little reason to trust anyone. They've been hurt so often by so many people that their walls of self-defense are almost impenetrable. They act tough and pretend that they're self-sufficient. They communicate that they don't need to be loved. But they do.

Your students need to know that even if they feel they can't trust anyone, they can trust God. He is the same yesterday, today, and forever. He will never leave them nor forsake them. He can be trusted, and he loves them.

This study focuses on the reasons that junior high teenagers can trust God. It will help teenagers begin to take small steps of faith. They can see that God will always prove faithful. And once they begin, they'll find it's easier to trust him again and again. In this study, teenagers will walk through Gideon's story and learn how he developed trust in God. They'll examine their own trust levels in God and others and investigate God's trustworthy character.

Through this exploration, teenagers can discover that God has impeccable character and that he is worthy of complete, childlike trust and faith.

The Point

▶ You can trust God.

Scripture Source

Leviticus 11:45; 2 Samuel 22:3; Proverbs 3:5-6; Acts 17:24-25; 1 John 4:7-10
These passages provide insights into God's character.

Judges 6:11-24, 33-40; 7:1-22
These passages describe the growth of Gideon's faith.

Hebrews 11:1
This verse describes faith.

The Study at a Glance

Warm-Up (10-15 minutes)

Baby Steps
What students will do: Indicate levels of trust by taking small or large steps.
Needs: ❏ masking tape

Bible Connection (30-35 minutes)

Faith Journey
What students will do:
Step 1 Compare God's attributes with human attributes and take small steps to the next activity.
Needs: ❏ Bibles ❏ newsprint
❏ markers ❏ twine
❏ scissors
Step 2 Rank situations in which it's hard for them to trust God and take larger steps to the next activity.
Needs: ❏ Bibles ❏ markers
❏ scissors ❏ paper
❏ pencils
Step 3 Brainstorm a list of baby steps to begin trusting God and take steps to the next activity.
Needs: ❏ Bibles ❏ markers
❏ paper ❏ pencils

Life Application (5-10 minutes)

The Finish Line
What students will do: Demonstrate levels of trust by leaning against one another and recognizing trustworthiness in one another.
Needs: ❏ Bibles ❏ marker

Optional Activity
What students will do: Write about concerns and questions on their own "fleece" and prayerfully commit to trust God.
Needs: ❏ 1 piece of felt ❏ fabric markers
(at least 6 inches square) per student

Before the Study →

For "Baby Steps," place a strip of masking tape along the floor in the center of the room to indicate a starting line.

For the Bible Connection and Life Application activities, hang four sheets of newsprint around the room to designate four stations. Write one of the four following labels on each of the sheets: "Step 1: Who Are You, God?" "Step 2: You Want Me to Do What?" "Step 3: Faith Steps," and "The Finish Line." Provide several Bibles and markers at each station.

If you choose to do the Optional Activity, gather or cut apart pieces of felt so that each student can have one. Felt pieces should be at least 6 inches square. Set out enough fabric markers so that each student can have one.

Warm-Up

Baby Steps
(10 to 15 minutes)

Begin by asking students to stand side by side behind the masking tape starting line you created.

SAY:

- I'm going to read a series of statements. After each statement, if you agree, take a small step forward. If you think the statement is false, take a giant step backward.

Read the following statements and allow students to take the appropriate steps:

- I think that people are generally trustworthy.
- I can trust my parents.
- I can trust my friends.
- I usually trust people, unless I have good reason not to.
- I think that people involved in organizations such as police or fire departments or churches are typically trustworthy.
- I can trust myself.
- I've never been hurt by someone breaking my trust.
- I think that other people trust me.
- I tend to believe people who say that I can trust them.
- I can trust God.

FYI Help your students think more deeply about their own spiritual journey by having them commit to keeping a journal for two months. Check out the suggested journaling plan explained in the "Changed 4 Life" section (p. 46) for specific ideas.

SAY:
- Take a look at how far you've moved from your original position.

ASK:
- What does your current position tell you about yourself? Explain.
- Is it good to be a trusting person? Why or why not?
- What does it mean to trust someone?
- How do you decide whether or not to trust someone?

Ask each student to find a partner.

SAY:
- Share with your partner one time that someone broke your trust or a time when you broke someone else's trust. Then tell your partner about one person you think you can trust and why you trust him or her.

When students have had time to share,

SAY:
- Many of us have been hurt so often that we've learned that it isn't safe to trust others. Having someone break your trust can be extremely painful. To protect ourselves from that pain, we build walls to keep others from finding out who we really are. We pretend to be tough, we laugh off put-downs, or we just don't admit that we might need someone we can be vulnerable with. God understands the pain we've been through, and he promises that he loves us and wants the best for us. Even when you feel as if you can't trust anyone, you can trust God.

◀ The Point

> **FYI**
> If you can, provide plenty of space for the "Baby Steps" activity. You might also give teenagers boundaries so they don't "giant step" right out of the classroom.

Faith Journey
(30 to 35 minutes)

Bible Connection

Step 1
Pass out twine and scissors to teenagers. Have each student cut a piece of twine that is equal to the length of his or her arm from shoulder to finger. Then have each student cut a piece of twine that is equal to the length of his or her leg from hip to foot. Ask students to

put the pieces of twine into their pockets for later use.

Have students form groups of four, then have them gather at the newsprint labeled "Step 1: Who Are You, God?" Ask someone to read aloud Judges 6:11-24 while others follow along.

SAY:

The Point ▶ ■ You can trust God, but most people don't usually learn to trust him all at once. Gideon learned to trust God by taking baby steps of faith, and his first step was to be sure that he was talking to God.

Assign each group one of the following passages: Leviticus 11:45; 2 Samuel 22:3; Acts 17:24-25; and 1 John 4:7-10.

SAY:

■ You have to know who God is in order to trust him. In your groups, read the passage, discuss what characteristics of God it describes, and then come up with a statement that contrasts who God is with who humans are. For example, if God is trustworthy because he is strong, you might say that God's strength is a chain, but man's strength is a Slinky; or God's strength is a tree trunk, but man's strength is a twig. When you have your statement, send one person from your group to write it on the newsprint.

Give groups about three minutes to read the passages and write their statements. Ask each group to explain what they discovered to the rest of the class.

ASK:

■ What would help you to have more trust in God?
■ How can knowing more about who God is help you to trust him?
■ What are some ways that you can learn more about God?

SAY:

The Point ▶ ■ One of the great things about God is that you can trust God with your life. He'll never let you down. And each time you exercise trust in him, it gets easier to trust him the next time.

Ask the teenagers to use the shorter lengths of twine that they cut to tie their ankles together.

FYI To increase participation and enthusiasm, consider tying your own ankles with twine as you walk from station to station.

SAY:
■ We're going to take small steps over to the next piece of newsprint. As you walk, try not to break the twine around your ankles.

Lead groups to the newsprint entitled "Step 2: You Want Me to Do What?"

ASK:
■ How are the steps you took over here like the first steps of faith Gideon was taking? How are they different?
■ Was it difficult to walk that way?
■ Is it difficult to trust God?

Have students remove the twine from their ankles.

Step 2
Ask someone to read aloud Judges 6:33-40 while others follow along. Give each group a sheet of paper and a pencil.

SAY:
■ Gideon began to trust God by doing what God asked of him, but before he went too far, he checked back with God to be sure that he'd heard correctly. With your group, brainstorm a list of five to seven situations where it is hard for you to trust God. When you have your list, rank the situations in order, with "one" being the situation where it is hardest for you to trust God. Write your top three situations on the newsprint, and then pray together that <u>you can trust God</u> in all areas of your lives. ◀ **The Point**

After groups have prayed together, have students tie their ankles together with their longer lengths of twine and step over to the newsprint entitled "Step 3: Faith Steps." Ask students to try to keep the twine from falling off their ankles as they walk.

ASK:
■ How is the twine around our ankles like our trust level in God? How is it different?
■ What larger steps of faith did Gideon begin to take?
■ Why do you think he took those steps of faith?
■ Have you seen your trust in God grow or diminish over the last year? Explain.

Have students remove the twine from their ankles.

FYI

If the twine breaks while teenagers are walking from station to station, don't worry. Use the event to show how God wants us to break into a higher level of trust in him. To do this ask questions such as:
■ How was breaking the twine while you walked like finding greater trust in God?
■ How was it different?

Step 3

Ask someone to read aloud Judges 7:1-8 while others follow along. Pass out a clean sheet of paper and a pencil to each group.

SAY:

- Gideon had to take baby steps before he had enough faith to allow God to reduce his army to almost nothing compared to the size of the enemy's army. In your groups, brainstorm a list of baby steps you can take to begin to trust God more. You might want to use one of the situations you ranked at the last station, and brainstorm baby steps for it. For example, if you said that it's hardest to trust God with your family, you might choose to trust that God is working with them and try being patient with them while he works. When you've come up with five to eight baby steps, write one or two baby steps on the newsprint and share it with the rest of the group.

SAY:

- Before moving to the next station, pair up with one person from your group and read Hebrews 11:1 together.

When students have read the verse,

ASK:

- What does this verse tell us about faith?
- How are faith and trust similar?
- Why is it important for Christians to have faith?
- Is it easy or hard for you to have faith in God? Explain.
- What do you think you can do to make your faith stronger?

SAY:

- Having faith in God isn't always easy, but without faith, we can't function as Christians. <u>You can trust God</u>, even if you have to start by taking baby steps. We've got one more station. Stay with your partner while we move over there to learn about the consequences of trusting God.

Have teenagers move to the newsprint marked "The Finish Line" without tying their ankles.

> **The Point ▶**

FYI

This would be a great opportunity for you to share with students something from your own life. Let teenagers know about a time in your faith journey during which you found it difficult to trust God. Perhaps a tragedy, death, or challenging circumstance really put your faith to the test, or maybe a particular Bible passage was difficult for you to understand. By talking freely with students about your faith ups and downs, you will help them be better prepared for the rough terrain they may face in their own spiritual lives.

ASK:

- Would you say your current trust in God is like walking with your ankles tied with the short twine, the long twine, or no twine at all?
- How does your trust in God compare to Gideon's trust in God? Explain.

The Finish Line
(5 to 10 minutes)

Life Application

Have students assemble at the newsprint marked "The Finish Line." Ask someone to read aloud Judges 7:9-22 while others follow along.

SAY:

- <u>You can trust God</u> and he will watch over you. Because Gideon trusted God, God promised him victory even before the battle began. Now stand back-to-back with your partner, shoulders touching.

◄ The Point

Allow students a moment to get in position.

SAY:

- Slowly step away from your partner, keeping your shoulders touching, until you're leaning on each other for support. Stay in that position while I read Proverbs 3:5-6.

FYI You may want to try this activity with someone about your own size before beginning the lesson so that you can accurately explain how far the students can safely walk away from each other. In order to prevent accidents, stress the importance of being a trustworthy friend to the teenagers before you have them do this activity. Don't require students to participate if they're hesitant or uncomfortable.

Read the verses, then

ASK:

- Do you like being in that position? Why or why not?
- How is leaning on your partner like leaning on your own understanding? How is it different?

- How is leaning on your partner like trusting God? How is it different?
- What would happen if your partner didn't lean back on you?
- What do you think it means to trust with all your heart?
- What are some things you can do to trust God with all your heart?
- When should we trust others? When shouldn't we?

SAY:

- God promises that when we trust him with all our hearts, he will give us success. Before you stand up straight, tell your partner one way that he or she is trustworthy. For example, you may say, "I know you're trustworthy because you don't gossip about others."

The Point ▶ While students talk, write "You can trust God with all your heart!" on the newsprint.

*Optional Activity

(up to 10 minutes)

Instead of "The Finish Line," try this activity.

Have students assemble at the newsprint marked "The Finish Line." Ask someone to read aloud Judges 7:9-22 while others follow along.

SAY:

> **The Point ▶** ■ <u>You can trust God</u>, and he will watch over you. Because Gideon trusted God, God promised him victory even before the battle began.

Invite a student to read aloud Proverbs 3:5-6 as you pass out a piece of felt and a fabric marker to each student.

SAY:

> ■ **This verse teaches us that we should trust in God with our whole hearts and not just rely on the way we understand things. But sometimes that's hard. Sometimes we have questions about God, about situations, about things we've seen or experienced, that make it hard for us to fully trust God.**

Invite teenagers to take a few moments to silently think of some questions, concerns, or doubts they've experienced that have made it difficult for them to fully trust God in everyday life situations. Then prompt teenagers to write a few words or draw a symbol on their piece of felt to represent their questions.

SAY:

> ■ **Gideon laid out his fleece because he wasn't quite sure—he needed some confirmation from God. God provided that confirmation.**
> **Think of your piece of fabric as your own fleece—your way of saying to God, "I trust you, but I'm not totally sure about something. Please show yourself to me and help me trust you more."**

Conclude by inviting teenagers to spread out around the room and take a few minutes to silently pray about what they wrote on their fleece, asking God to help them grow in their ability to trust him. Encourage students to take their piece of fabric with them as a reminder to pray about that issue on a regular basis.

Guided by God

Study 2

Imagine what life in Metropolis would've been like if Clark Kent just led a normal life. He didn't do anything out of the ordinary. He just went through life, day to day. Why? Not because he didn't care about those in need—because he didn't *know* he had superpowers.

Wow, that would sure be a waste!

That's how many Christians live day to day. They go through ordinary life. They face choices and challenges. And they do it all without employing the help of the amazing power within them: the presence of the Holy Spirit.

In this study, your junior highers will discover that, if they are Christians, God's Spirit lives within them! The Holy Spirit can guide them through all of the difficult decisions they face in life. They'll learn that they've got something amazing, unmatched even by the likes of Superman!

The Point

▶ The Holy Spirit lives within you.

Scripture Source

John 14:15-17
Jesus promises that God the Father will send the Holy Spirit to live in those who follow Jesus.

Romans 8:9-11
Paul explains that those who believe in Jesus have the Holy Spirit living in them and giving them life.

1 Corinthians 2:10-16
Paul writes that the Holy Spirit helps Christians understand spiritual truths.

Galatians 3:1-5; Titus 3:4-7
These passages explain that the Holy Spirit is a gift of grace given to those who believe that Jesus died and rose from the dead for them.

The Study at a Glance

Warm-Up (10-15 minutes)

Is This You?
What students will do: Create descriptions of each other and try to figure out who's describing them.

Needs: ❏ slips of paper ❏ pencils

Bible Connection (30-35 minutes)

Life Within
What students will do: Act out a scene about the Holy Spirit living within them by using puppets they've created.

Needs:
❏ Bibles
❏ photocopies of "Life Within" instructions (p. 24)
❏ paper sacks
❏ socks
❏ material scraps
❏ buttons
❏ craft sticks
❏ yarn
❏ straws
❏ cardboard
❏ foil
❏ markers
❏ construction paper
❏ scissors
❏ glue
❏ long rectangular table
❏ pipe cleaners

Bonus Activity (10-15 minutes)

What students will do: Look up additional Scripture passages about the role the Holy Spirit plays in their lives and display what they learned.

Needs:
❏ Bibles
❏ photocopies of "Who Is the Holy Spirit Anyway?" (p. 24)
❏ markers
❏ scissors
❏ paper (or construction paper)
❏ tape

Life Application (5-10 minutes)

Puppet Prayers
What students will do: Pray about how they can experience the Holy Spirit living within them.

Needs: ❏ Bibles ❏ markers
❏ puppets from "Life Within" activity

Before the Study

For the Bible Connection activity, gather lots of creative puppet-making supplies such as old (washed) socks, brown paper sacks, material scraps, buttons, craft sticks, yarn, pipe cleaners, straws, cardboard, foil, markers, construction paper, scissors, and glue. You'll also need one long rectangular table that you should lay on its side as a makeshift puppet stage. Make one photocopy of the "Life Within" instructions (p. 24) for every eighteen students in your group. Cut the sets of instructions apart so each group of six students will have one set.

If you decide to do the Bonus Activity, you'll also need to make at least one photocopy of the "Who Is the Holy Spirit Anyway?" handout (p. 24) and cut apart the slips. If you have more than sixteen students, you'll need to make additional copies.

Warm-Up

Is This You?
(10 to 15 minutes)

Hand each student a slip of paper and a pencil. Have students write down their names, then collect the slips and redistribute them. Make sure no one chooses a slip that has his or her own name on it.

SAY:

- Your job is to write a description of the person whose name is on the slip of paper. Don't let anyone know who you're writing about. To accomplish this, list things you already know about the person and ask questions of others in the group. For example, if you're supposed to find out information about someone named Allison, you could ask, "What are Jeremy's, Allison's, and Curtis' favorite colors?" As you write your description, avoid referring to your person's name or gender. Remember, don't let anyone know who you're describing.

Allow teenagers three minutes to create their descriptions. Then have the group sit in a circle while each person reads the description he or she wrote. When everyone is finished, have teenagers each guess who wrote about them.

Then have teenagers form trios to discuss these questions:

FYI: You may have teenagers in your class who aren't Christians and don't relate to the Holy Spirit. That's OK. Accept them for who they are. Remember that even if some students don't show interest in this study, you're planting seeds that may someday sprout into a relationship with Christ.

- How did you know who wrote a description of you?
- Did the description of you match how you'd describe yourself? Explain.
- Was the term *Christian* used to describe you? Why do you think it was or wasn't?
- If you were to write a description of yourself, would you use the word *Christian*? Why or why not?

The Point ▶
- If you're a Christian, are you aware that <u>the Holy Spirit lives within you</u>? Why or why not? Or if you're not a Christian, what do you think of the idea that the Holy Spirit will live in you if you believe that Jesus died to give you eternal life?

When trios have finished discussing the questions,

SAY:

- The Bible says that if you're a Christian, <u>the Holy Spirit lives within you</u>. As a believer in Jesus, you have God's very presence living inside of you to comfort you, counsel you, and guide you. We're going to explore what that means in the next activity. ◀ **The Point**

> **FYI**
> In addition to gathering materials and preparing your room, pray that the Holy Spirit will work through you to reach the hearts and minds of your young people with his truth.

Life Within
(30 to 35 minutes)

Bible Connection

Have each trio find another trio to create a group of six. Hand each group one of the three "Life Within" instructions.

SAY:

- The Bible expresses how the Holy Spirit lives in us when we become Christians. On this handout is a Scripture and a situation you might face in your life. In your group, pray that God will use your Bible passage to teach you how <u>the Holy Spirit lives within you</u>. Look closely at what the Bible says about the role the Holy Spirit plays in your life. Then create a short puppet show, acting out your solution based on your Scripture passage. I've provided some materials you can use to create your puppets. The only catch is that you can't work your puppets with your hands. You can use your feet, elbows, knees—anything but your hands. You have twenty minutes to prepare your puppet show. ◀ **The Point**

Direct students' attention to the table piled high with puppet-making supplies and let them get started.

FYI

Let students get goofy! Junior highers *won't* like the idea of making puppets and doing a puppet show if they get the impression that you expect this to be a "serious" activity. But if they get the drift that the activity is not only supposed to be meaningful but also should be funny, silly, and full of laughs, they're bound to have fun! Remember, your attitude will set the tone for participants in the study, so don't be afraid to make a bizarre-looking puppet yourself!

FYI

If your teenagers are interested, have them practice their puppet shows and perform them at other church functions such as children's church or before a sermon about the Holy Spirit.

When groups are ready, have them present their short puppet shows. Then have teenagers return to their trios and express one thing they learned from each other's puppet shows.

Then have trios discuss these questions:

- How easy was it to work your puppet without your hands?
- How was working your puppet without your hands like living your life without the Holy Spirit guiding you? How was it different?
- How was working your puppet with other parts of your body like allowing spiritual influences other than the Holy Spirit to guide you? How was it different?

Invite a student in each trio to read Romans 8:9-11, then

ASK:
- What does this passage say about how the Holy Spirit can live in you? about how his presence affects you?
- Are you a Christian? If so, how have you experienced the Holy Spirit within you? If not, would you like the Holy Spirit to live in you? Explain.

When trios have finished their discussion, invite students to express to the class their thoughts and feelings about any of the questions they've just discussed. Tell the group:

- Just as you made your puppet come to life, when you have a lifelong relationship with Jesus Christ, <u>the Holy Spirit lives within you.</u> The Holy Spirit ◄ **The Point** gives you new life and can serve as your guide in all of the decisions you'll make and the challenges you'll face throughout the rest of your life.

Bonus Activity

(10 to 15 minutes)

If you have time, try this activity after "Life Within."

Pass out one slip from "Who Is the Holy Spirit Anyway?" (p. 24) to each student.

SAY:
- **We've just touched the tip of the iceberg when it comes to what we can learn about the Holy Spirit! Let's take a few minutes to get to know the Holy Spirit even better.**

Have teenagers look up the Scripture passages on their slips of paper. Tell them to look for one basic fact or idea they can learn about the Holy Spirit from the Bible passage.

Set a pile of markers, scissors, tape, and paper in the middle of the room and explain that teenagers will use these supplies to each create a simple "billboard" advertising what they learned about the Holy Spirit. They should write a sentence summarizing their main point, beginning with "The Holy Spirit is..." Then they should decorate their paper and cut it into a unique shape.

Once they've finished working on their papers, prompt them to use tape to post their paper "billboards" on the puppet stage. When all the papers are posted, invite students to each read their sentence aloud so that everyone can benefit from what they studied.

ASK:
- **What is one new thing about the Holy Spirit that you learned from this activity?**
- **How does it make you feel to know that God offers you so much help in your everyday life?**

 If you have less than sixteen students, give some students two or more slips of paper. If you have more than sixteen students, make additional photocopies of the handout so that each student gets one slip. In that instance, have teenagers gather together in pairs or trios with the other students who have the same Bible passage and work together to create their "billboard."

Life Application | Puppet Prayers
(5 to 10 minutes)

Have teenagers scatter throughout the room, keeping their puppets with them. Set out markers for teenagers to use.

SAY:

The Point ▶

- If you're a Christian, <u>the Holy Spirit lives within you</u>. If you're not, you can accept this source of life if you wish. Either way, take a few moments to read Titus 3:4-7 and pray about your relationship with God. Write on your puppet anything you hear from God about your relationship—assurances he gives you that the Holy Spirit lives within you, ideas he gives you about living out your relationship with him, or any commitments he wants you to make. Then write one way you'll respond to what you've learned today. For example, you might spend five minutes in prayer every day for the next week. Or you might explore more about the Holy Spirit in your Bible.

Allow teenagers three minutes for their prayer time. Before you dismiss the students, encourage teenagers to take their puppets home to remind them that the Holy Spirit lives within them.

Life Within
Instructions

Read John 14:15-17 and create a puppet show that expresses your answer to this question:

■ How would believing this passage affect your response to a friend who wanted you to give in to peer pressure?

Read 1 Corinthians 2:10-16 and create a puppet show that expresses your answer to this question:

■ How would believing this passage affect your response to a friend who felt torn between going to a youth group lock-in or going to a party in which drugs and alcohol would be used?

Read Galatians 3:1-5 and create a puppet show that expresses your answer to this question:

■ How would believing this passage affect your response to a Christian friend afraid of losing the Holy Spirit because he or she engaged in premarital sex?

Who Is the Holy Spirit Anyway?

Cut apart these slips and give one to each student in your group.

Psalm 139:7-10

Luke 1:35

John 7:37-39

John 14:26

John 15:26

John 16:8-11

Acts 5:1-4

Acts 9:31

Romans 8:9-13

Romans 8:26-27

1 Corinthians 2:10-12

1 Corinthians 12:4-7

Ephesians 2:19-22

2 Thessalonians 2:13

Hebrews 9:14

2 Peter 1:21

Everyday Grace

Sports, school, music, TV, jobs, dates, youth group—today's teenagers have busy, and seemingly full, lives. Some of the activities are positive, some are negative. All of them, though, fail to fill the void many teenagers are trying so hard to satisfy. The things many young people pursue to gain peace and contentment just leave them feeling more empty.

Only Jesus can fill the void in the human heart. Today's teenagers desperately need to hear of the grace and fulfillment he extends to them. Teenagers need to learn that Jesus has paid the price for the wrong things they've done and for the sins they continue to struggle with each day. Because Jesus has taken the penalty for their sin, teenagers who accept God's grace can have the peace with God they long for.

This study provides an opportunity for teenagers to discover the grace of Jesus as it relates to salvation and to the everyday trials they face.

The Point

▶ We need to rely on God's grace every day.

Scripture Source

Exodus 20:1-17; Matthew 22:34-40; James 2:10
These passages describe God's laws for our behavior.

Genesis 3:1-24; Matthew 5:21-24; Romans 3:10-18, 23
These passages talk about our guilt and the sinful state we're in.

Genesis 1:26-31; Psalm 139:13-16; Isaiah 55:8-9
These passages talk about God's sovereignty in our lives.

John 3:14-21; Romans 6:22-23; 8:1-6
These passages talk about the forgiveness and eternal life made possible through Jesus' sacrifice on our behalf.

Ephesians 2:8
This verse explains that we are saved by grace through faith.

The Study at a Glance

Warm-Up (5-10 minutes)

Briefing
What students will do: Create balloon self-portraits and receive roles and instructions for investigating the guilt of humanity before God.
Needs: ❏ Bibles ❏ balloons
❏ markers ❏ "Role" handouts (pp. 34-35)

Bible Connection (30-40 minutes)

The Trial
What students will do: Investigate Scriptures and present evidence about the guilt of humanity before God. Students will also summarize their arguments and talk about judgment and grace as they pop their balloon self-portraits.
Needs: ❏ Bibles ❏ "Role" handouts
❏ paper (pp. 34-35)
❏ pencils ❏ paper clips
❏ balloons from Warm-Up

Life Application (up to 10 minutes)

Court Reporters
What students will do: Create pictures or words for display that represent everyday trials they face.
Needs: ❏ blank overhead transparencies
❏ markers ❏ overhead projector

Before the Study →

Photocopy and cut out the "Role" handouts (pp. 34-35). Make enough copies so that each person in a group will have one handout and each handout will be given to roughly the same number of people. Fold and staple or tape each handout so that only the role at the top is showing.

On separate slips of paper, write "Ephesians 2:8." Put each slip inside a deflated balloon for each student in class.

Warm-Up

Briefing
(5 to 10 minutes)

As teenagers arrive, give each of them a balloon with the Bible verse inside it. Ask teenagers to blow up the balloons and tie them off, leaving the paper inside their balloons. Set the markers in the middle of the room.

SAY:

- I'd like you to use your balloon and a marker to create a self-portrait. Draw something on your balloon that's representative of who you are. You can draw a face, a symbol, a scene—anything that represents *you*.

When teenagers finish,

SAY:

- Today we're going to conduct a trial. Our defendant is humanity. Humanity is charged with breaking God's law and causing lives to be empty and sinful. Since you're a part of humanity, you're on trial too. Your balloon will serve as a reminder of that fact.

If you have extra chairs, have teenagers line the chairs up against a wall and put their balloons in the chairs. If you don't have extra chairs, have teenagers set their balloons against a wall for later use.

Have students form four equal groups: the Law, the Prosecution, the Defense Attorneys, and the Witnesses. Give each person a "Role" handout (pp. 34-35) according to the group he or she is part of. Be sure to tell students to keep their handouts folded until you say it's OK to open them. Also make sure each group has at least one Bible.

SAY:

- Each one of you has been assigned to a group based on a role you'll play in the trial. You'll have ten minutes to read the handouts I've given you, gather your evidence, and formulate your cases. Then we'll hold the trial. Each group will have a chance to present its evidence, then respond to what other groups say. During the trial, we'll be examining how <u>we</u> ◀ **The Point** <u>need to rely on God's grace every day</u>.

The Trial
(30 to 40 minutes)

Give each group paper and pencils. Give groups ten minutes to read the handouts, follow the directions, do the research, and prepare their cases.

After ten minutes,

SAY:

- Court is now in session. I am your honorable judge presiding. Would the members of the Law please stand?

When the members of the Law have stood,

SAY:

- You have three minutes to present your case. Please tell the court the position of the Law.

To help the members of the Law present their group's position, ask the following questions as necessary:

- What is the Law that God expects humanity to live up to?
- Do you have evidence to present to the court?
- Does the Law allow for any exceptions or loopholes?
- What does it take for someone to be labeled as a law-breaker?
- What are the immediate and eternal consequences of breaking the Law?

When the Law has finished presenting its case,

Bible Connection

FYI

In every group of younger teenagers, there are usually at least a few who have a difficult time staying on task, especially when they're asked to work on something without the direction of a leader or adult. While teenagers are working on their handouts and doing research during this activity, wander from group to group and encourage students to stay focused on their assignment. Pay special attention to teenagers who need some extra prodding and work alongside them if needed.

SAY:

- Thank you. Now we will hear from the Prosecution. Would the members of the Prosecution please stand?

When the members of the Prosecution have stood,

SAY:

- You have three minutes to present your case. Please tell the court the position of the Prosecution.

To help the Prosecution present their group's position, ask the following questions as necessary:

- Has the defendant broken the Law?
- Do you have any evidence to present to the court?
- How has breaking the Law affected humanity?
- What is the punishment for breaking the Law?
- What do you think the defendant deserves?

When the Prosecution has finished presenting its case,

SAY:

- Thank you. Now we will hear from the Defense Attorneys. Would the Defense Attorneys please stand?

When the Defense Attorneys have stood,

SAY:

- You have three minutes to present your case. Please tell the court the position of the Defense Attorneys.

To help the Defense Attorneys present their group's position, ask the following questions:

- How does the defendant plead: guilty or not guilty?
- Do you have any evidence to present to the court?
- Is there anything the court should know about your client that hasn't already been pointed out?
- Do you think your client deserves what the Prosecution says?

When the Defense Attorneys have finished presenting their case,

SAY:

- Thank you. Now we will hear from the Witnesses. Would the Witnesses please stand?

When the Witnesses have stood,

SAY:

- You have three minutes to present your case. Please tell the court the position of the Witnesses.

To help the Witnesses present their group's position, ask the following questions:

- Do you believe the defendant is guilty or not guilty?
- Do you have any evidence to present to the court?
- Do you believe the defendant should be punished? Why or why not?
- What do the defendant's actions, both good and bad, have to do with your testimony?
- How has grace affected humanity?

When the Witnesses have finished presenting their case,

SAY:

- Thank you. You may take your seat. We've heard from the Law regarding the standards humanity is required to live up to. The Prosecution has told us what humanity has done wrong. The Defense Attorneys have stated their case as to why humanity should not be convicted. The Witnesses have shared their shocking information, proving that no matter how many good or bad things humanity does, life is empty without Jesus. As we move on to the next phase of our trial, start thinking about how this activity helps us understand that <u>we need to rely on God's grace every day</u>. ◀ **The Point**

    We'll now take a short recess while each group prepares its final arguments. During this time, prepare to give your final statements to win your case. Every group will have an opportunity to speak during the final arguments.

As teenagers prepare their final arguments, move from group to group, offering direction to teenagers who need help in preparing summaries of their viewpoints.

After a few minutes,

ASK:

- Does anyone have any new information to share?
- Members of the Law, according to your evidence, what kind of life did God intend for humanity to have?

- Members of the Prosecution, according to your evidence, what is the cause of the emptiness of life for much of humanity?
- Defense Attorneys, what are some things that humanity uses to try to fill the emptiness of life?
- Witnesses, how does Jesus' grace remedy the emptiness of life? Does having a full life mean a person is always happy? Why or why not?
- Who believes the defendant is guilty as charged?
- Who believes the defendant should be punished?
- What punishment should the defendant receive?

Give each student a paper clip. Ask teenagers to get their balloons and hold on to them.

SAY:

- We all deserve to be punished for our sin. We deserve eternal separation from God. To symbolize this, please pop your balloon with the end of your paper clip.

After teenagers have popped their balloons,

ASK:

- Was it difficult to pop your balloon?
- How is this like the punishment we deserve for our sin? How is it different?
- Are the consequences of sin fair? Explain.

Ask a volunteer to look up the Bible verse that is written on the paper in his or her balloon and read it aloud.

ASK:

- According to Ephesians 2:8 and the information the Witnesses have shared with us, what is the factor that determines whether humanity is punished or set free?
- Do you think this is fair? Explain.
- According to the things we've learned in this trial, what would you say is the definition of *grace*? What is the opposite of grace?
- How does knowing Jesus affect our present circumstances?

The Point ▶
- What evidence have we discussed that demonstrates <u>we need to rely on God's grace every day</u>?

SAY:

- It's important for us to understand how the results of this trial apply to our everyday lives. Please take home your Bible verse as a reminder of the grace that's found in Jesus. Right now, we're going to take a look at how that grace can make our lives complete.

Court Reporters
(up to 10 minutes)

Life Application

Give each person a blank overhead transparency and a marker.

SAY:

- On this transparency, draw or write something that represents everyday trials you are experiencing. For example, you may choose to show how you feel "prosecuted" by standards and pressures, or you may want to show expectations and how you feel that you fail to live up to them. You'll have five minutes to create your transparencies. Then you'll present your pictures or words to each other. Please sign your name on your transparency.

After five minutes,

SAY:

- As we look at the drawings or words you've created, think about ways God's grace can help you through these situations.

Ask each student to trade transparencies with someone else in the room. Have each student write one word on the transparency that symbolizes how God's grace is at work in the life of that person. For example, a student may write "joyful" on a transparency because God's joy is shown in that person's life. Then collect the transparencies and show them on an overhead projector. Allow students to describe or explain their pictures if they want to.

When you have displayed the students' creations,

ASK:

- What are some ways God's grace can help you through these everyday trials?

FYI

If you have access to a slide projector, you may want to provide teenagers with blank slides and fine-point markers and present a slide show instead. If you don't have access to a slide projector or an overhead projector, you may want to have teenagers create their drawings or words on sheets of paper, put the papers in a stack, and display each sheet by slowly flipping through the stack.

■ How can you respond to God's grace in these everyday situations?

SAY:

The Point ▶ ■ Through Jesus' grace our lives can be full. <u>We need to rely on God's grace every day</u> in every circumstance.

Pray a prayer similar to this one:

■ Dear God, I pray that you will reveal yourself to all of us and make it clear to each one of us that your grace is at work in our lives. Please give us the courage to respond to your grace on a daily basis. As we realize how much you have done for us, teach us to accept your free gift and to live as your children. Amen.

Role: The Law

INSTRUCTIONS

1. Do your research. As the Law, you are responsible for looking up and pointing out the standards for human behavior. Use the "Evidence" section below to help you gather information by reading the Bible verses, discussing the questions that follow, and using your answers to strengthen your case.

2. Prepare your presentation. Be sure to assert yourselves, constantly making the point that the Law speaks for itself in the midst of arguments and excuses from the Defense Attorneys. Use the "Tips" section below to help you prepare an effective presentation.

EVIDENCE

Exodus 20:1-17
- Why do you think God made these laws?
- Would a person have a fulfilled life if he or she kept all these laws? Why or why not?

Matthew 22:34-40
- Why do you think these two commands are the most important ones?
- How would the world be different if humanity always obeyed these two laws?

James 2:10
- Why does breaking one command make a person guilty of breaking all the commands?

TIPS

- Be prepared to tell the court what God requires of humanity.
- Try to summarize some of the most important laws.
- Make it very clear that the Law allows for no exceptions.
- Explain the immediate and eternal consequences for breaking some or all of the laws.

Role: The Prosecution

INSTRUCTIONS

1. Do your research. As the Prosecution, you are responsible for presenting evidence that the defendant, humanity, has broken the Law. Use the "Evidence" section below to help you gather information by reading the Bible verses, discussing the questions that follow, and using your answers to strengthen your case.

2. Prepare your presentation. Be sure to point to the Law as the ultimate standard, constantly making the point that the evidence speaks for itself in the midst of arguments and excuses from the Defense Attorneys. Use the "Tips" section below to help you prepare an effective presentation.

EVIDENCE

Genesis 3:1-24
- What effect did Adam and Eve's sin have on humanity?
- Why do we *all* have to pay for Adam and Eve's sin?

Romans 3:10-18, 23
- Who is guilty of being a lawbreaker?
- What are the immediate consequences of breaking God's law?

Matthew 5:21-22
- What does it take to break God's law?
- What are the eternal consequences of breaking God's law?

TIPS

- Determine and point out the proper punishment for those who break the Law.
- Don't allow the Defense Attorneys to make excuses—if people break the Law, they're guilty.
- Remind the court that breaking one law is just as bad as breaking all the laws. Lawbreakers deserve punishment.
- Point out that because humanity is self-centered and disobedient to God, life has become empty and meaningless. This is not what God intended for humanity when he created Adam and Eve.

Permission to photocopy this handout from Faith 4 Life: Junior High Bible Study Series, *My Life as a Christian* granted for local church use. Copyright © Group Publishing, Inc., P.O. Box 481, Loveland, CO 80539. www.grouppublishing.com

Role: The Defense Attorneys

INSTRUCTIONS

1. Do your research. As the Defense Attorneys, you are responsible for defending humanity against the accusations of the Prosecution. Use the "Evidence" section below to help you gather information by reading the Bible verses, discussing the questions, and using your answers to strengthen your case.

2. Prepare your presentation. Be sure to emphasize the positive things humanity has done, constantly making the point that it's not fair to concentrate only on the negative things. Use the "Tips" section below to help you prepare an effective presentation.

EVIDENCE

Genesis 1:26-31
- How can people be lawbreakers if they're created in God's image?
- Are people basically good or basically bad? Explain.

Isaiah 55:8-9
- Is it possible to live up to God's standards?
- Does God really expect us to live up to his high standards?

Psalm 139:13-16
- Since God created us, doesn't he share the responsibility for our guilt?
- Can people be good without God?

TIPS

- Point out that God's laws are impossible to keep—God doesn't really expect people to be able to live up to them.
- Remind the court that your client is good at heart. Give some examples of wonderful things humanity has done that you think outweigh the bad. For example, humanity has fed the hungry, created amazing inventions and artwork, and gone to church for thousands of years. Your client is even made in the image of God.
- Don't forget that God created humanity, so he should hold some responsibility for humanity's actions.

Role: The Witnesses

INSTRUCTIONS

1. Do your research. As the Witnesses, you are responsible for introducing new evidence that could clear or convict the defendant, humanity, who is accused of breaking the Law. Use the "Evidence" section below to help you gather information by reading the Bible verses, discussing the questions, and using your answers to strengthen your case.

2. Prepare your presentation. Be sure to point to the grace of Jesus, constantly making the point that regardless of the defendant's guilt, the punishment has already been taken by someone else. Use the "Tips" section below to help you prepare an effective presentation.

EVIDENCE

John 3:14-21
- Why does belief in Jesus pardon people of their guilt? Is that fair?

Romans 6:22-23
- What can we do to earn pardon for our sins?
- Why did God give us the gift of eternal life?

Romans 8:1-6
- Does God's grace provide pardon for everyone's sins?
- What benefits come from accepting God's grace and following the Spirit?

TIPS

- Point out that the punishment for humanity's sin has already been paid.
- Determine what the requirements are for a defendant to be found innocent.
- Remind the court that through God's grace, people can receive pardon and escape the punishment they deserve for their sin.
- Tell everyone that Jesus' grace brings fullness to the meaningless lives of those who disobey God. Jesus is the remedy for the emptiness of life, no matter what the circumstances of humanity.

No Matter the Cost

Study 4

Being a Christian makes life a lot easier...right?

Wrong.

Whether they've heard it from you, from others, or have come to the conclusion themselves, the idea that being a Christian makes life easier is a prevalent perception in the minds of many teenagers. After all, doesn't being a Christian mean you get good grades? your family life is great? you have good friends? you succeed? bad things don't happen to you?

The Christians in the early church knew very well that following Christ is an entirely different story. Yes, life was better for them—they now had a purpose, a community, a relationship with the living God. But life *definitely* didn't get easier. Just ask Stephen, stoned to death for his faith in Christ. Or ask Paul, imprisoned, beaten, and left for dead because he claimed Christ as Lord.

Through this Bible study, junior highers will discover that followers of Jesus can expect to face persecution for their faith. They'll be inspired by biblical examples of early disciples and will be encouraged to endure suffering with perseverance.

The Point

▶ Following Jesus involves suffering for your faith.

Scripture Source

Matthew 5:10-12
Jesus blesses those who are persecuted for his sake.

Acts 6:8-15; 7:54-8:3
This passage describes the martyrdom of Stephen and the persecution of the early church.

2 Corinthians 11:23-29
Paul describes the many ways he has suffered as a follower of Christ.

2 Timothy 2:3
Paul encourages Timothy to endure hardship.

The Study at a Glance

Warm-Up (up to 10 minutes)

Danger Is My Name
What students will do: Have a volunteer recruit people for dangerous jobs.

Needs: ❑ "Profile and Job Openings" handout (p. 44)

Bonus Activity (15- 20 minutes)

What students will do: Experience what it feels like to take a risk by participating in an on-the-spot obstacle course.

Needs: ❑ blindfolds   ❑ treats
❑ classroom furniture

Bible Connection (20-25 minutes)

Hazardous Duty
What students will do: Read Scriptural examples of people being persecuted for their faith and discuss the risks of following Jesus.

Needs: ❑ Bibles
❑ "Hazardous Duty Warning" handout (p. 45)
❑ pencils

Life Application (15- 25 minutes)

Counting the Cost
What students will do: Consider the risks and rewards of following Christ and discuss times they've personally paid a price for their faith in Jesus.

Needs: ❑ index cards
❑ pencils
❑ CD of soft music
❑ CD player
❑ wooden or metal cross
❑ coins
❑ buckets

Before the Study →

For the Warm-Up activity, talk with a teenager before the study who you think would be willing to play the role of Duke or Diane Danger, the owner and president of Dangerous Jobs International. Photocopy the "Profile and Job Openings" handout (p. 44) and give a copy to the student so he or she can prepare ahead of time.

If you choose to do the Bonus Activity, prepare treats to share with your students, such as cookies or candy bars. You'll also need to collect several blindfolds.

For "Hazardous Duty," make several photocopies of the "Hazardous Duty Warning" handout (p. 45). You'll need one copy for every group of four teenagers.

For the Life Application activity, locate a wooden or metal cross that can stand up on a table. Set it on a table in a corner of your meeting room. Set up a CD player with a CD of soft music that you can play during this part of the study. Also, gather enough buckets so that every group of six or fewer students can use one. Fill each of these buckets with water. Finally, collect enough coins (pennies, nickels, dimes, or quarters) so that every teenager can have one.

Warm-Up | Danger Is My Name
(up to 10 minutes)

When students arrive, announce that a special guest from Dangerous Jobs International has come to interview candidates for placement in hazardous positions around the world. Invite the volunteer to make his or her presentation.

After Duke or Diane finishes "recruiting" teenagers,

ASK:
- Why would people want to do this kind of work?
- What would keep people from applying for this kind of work?
- What are the dangers associated with each job?
- Compared to the other jobs we discussed, would you describe following Jesus as a dangerous job? Why or why not?

Invite a teenager to read aloud Matthew 5:10-12, then

ASK:

- Based on what Jesus said in this passage, do any of you want to change your answer to the last question? Why or why not?
- What are the dangers associated with following Jesus?

SAY:

- Being a disciple of Jesus is a risky venture. <u>Following Jesus involves suffering for your faith.</u> ◀ **The Point** Let's take a closer look at what this means in our everyday lives.

> **FYI** Depending on where you live, it is quite possible that your students have never faced severe persecution for their faith in Christ. The discussions in this study offer a great opportunity for you to open teenagers' eyes to the reality of persecution that other Christians are facing in various parts of the world. Use resources such as Voice of the Martyrs magazine, news stories on www.christianitytoday.com, or information provided through your church or denomination to share specific examples of the extreme persecution (imprisonment, starvation, martyrdom, and so on) that other followers of Christ are currently facing.

Bonus Activity

(15 to 20 minutes)

If you have time, try this activity after "Danger Is My Name."

Blindfold two or three volunteers. Invite the remaining students to help you quickly set up a "Risk Route" by arranging tables and chairs in a complicated and seemingly difficult obstacle course.

Select a student to guide the volunteers through the course by voice instructions. Have the group respond to the volunteers' immediate circumstances by offering gasps, warnings and applause to enhance the atmosphere of danger. After students finish the course, have everyone applaud.

Repeat the activity a few more times with different volunteers. Each time, rearrange the tables and chairs to create new courses. Then award treats (such as fruit, donuts, or candy bars) to the people who made it through the course.

ASK the volunteers:

- How did you feel going through the course? Explain.
- How did you feel about your guide?

- How did the group's comments make you feel?
- How did you feel about the reward?

ASK the rest of the students:
- How did you see the danger differently than the volunteers?
- What did you think when the volunteers received their reward?

SAY:
- The risks of following Jesus are like the risks of the Risk Route. You don't always know what's coming up or what obstacles you'll face—but the reward of a closer relationship with God is always waiting at the other end of the risk. And while the Risk Route award lasts only a short time, your improved relationship with God lasts a lifetime.

FYI Though it doesn't seem "fair" to give treats only to some students, use this activity to demonstrate that the reward was for those who took the challenge. Explain that the activity is a parallel to following Christ: those who are followers of Christ face suffering and danger, but they also receive the great reward of a close relationship with God.

Bible Connection: Hazardous Duty
(20 to 25 minutes)

Invite teenagers to form groups of no more than four. Give groups each a "Hazardous Duty Warning" handout (p. 45), a pencil, and a Bible. Tell each group they're the Dangerous Duty Committee. Assign half of the groups to study Paul in 2 Corinthians 11:23-29 and the rest of the groups to study Stephen in Acts 6:8-15 and 7:54–8:3. Have students work on the handout together in their groups. Once they've finished, have each "Paul" group pair up with a "Stephen" group. Prompt them to share what they've written and add to their list anything they learned from the other group.

Once groups are done sharing with each other, have everyone join back together and

ASK:
- Why would the first Christians take these risks?
- How do you think they might have felt at the time?
- Do you think you'd be willing to go through what Paul and

Stephen went through because of your faith in Christ? Explain your thoughts and feelings.
- ■ Do you think you'll ever face situations like they did? Why or why not?
- ■ What are some of the risks Christians today face because of their faith in Christ?

SAY:

- ■ As we just learned, Paul went through a lot for his faith in Christ. When Paul neared the end of his life, he wrote a letter to Timothy, a young man he loved like a spiritual son.

Invite a volunteer to read aloud 2 Timothy 2:3, then

ASK:

- ■ What can you learn from this Scripture, knowing that these are some of Paul's "last words" to Timothy?

SAY:

- ■ Notice that Paul doesn't say, "*If* you face tough times," or "*Just in case* you encounter hardships." He says, "Endure hardships" matter-of-factly. He knows they're going to happen. Paul knows that <u>following Jesus involves suffering for your faith</u>. Like those we read about today, you may be laughed at, ignored, verbally or physically abused, or worse, for being a follower of Jesus. But the reward of a close relationship with God is worth all that pain and humiliation.

◄ **The Point**

Counting the Cost
(15 to 25 minutes)

Life Application

Distribute an index card and a pencil to each student. Play some soft music in the background and draw students' attention to the table on which you've placed a cross.

SAY:

- ■ This part of the study is between you and God—no one will ask you to tell what you write on your card—so don't sign your name. Across the top of one side of your card write "Rewards." Then list one or two rewards you get for being a Christian. (Pause.) Now across the top of the other side of

> **FYI**
> Try to select music that will add a worshipful ambience to this activity. A contemporary worship CD or an instrumental album would both work well.

the card write "Risks." List one or two things you're willing to risk to gain the rewards listed on the other side. (Pause.) Jesus never promised that following him would be easy, but he did promise that the cost would be worth the pain we might experience.

As the music continues to play, invite students each to show their willingness to risk for Jesus' sake by placing their cards on the table with the cross on it.

SAY:

■ Just as we place these cards on this table, we place our lives in God's hands. Let this moment be a time of commitment for each of us as we boldly step forward to face the cost of discipleship.

Have teenagers form groups of six or fewer. Have groups each form a circle. Give each teenager a coin, and place a bucket in the center of each circle.

SAY:

The Point ▶

■ When someone makes an investment in something, they count the cost. They understand the rewards, and they understand the price. As followers of Christ, we must count the cost. We must understand that <u>following Jesus involves suffering for our faith</u>.

Have teenagers each share one time they "paid a price" for their belief in Christ. Tell teenagers it's OK to be silent. After each person's turn, have him or her drop the coin into the bucket. Then have the rest of the teenagers in the circle say why they appreciate that person's willingness to be a follower of Jesus.

Have each group close in a time of silent prayer. Then have teenagers go around and challenge each other to be willing to risk for Jesus' sake by saying: "[Name], go out and be a bold follower of Jesus. With God's help, I know you can do it."

Profile and Job Openings

Duke or Diane Danger
Owner and president:
DANGEROUS JOBS INTERNATIONAL

You travel across the country to recruit teenagers for dangerous jobs worldwide. You're not afraid of danger.

In fact, you live for danger.

Introduce yourself to the class. Then describe your company, and tell the students about one or two of your dangerous assignments—like the time you were in Africa, surrounded by 50 hungry lions…

Then explain the following job openings. Do your best to convince teenagers to sign up for one of these jobs:

■ **WANTED:**
Hellfire Fighters to put out oil-rig fires by exploding dynamite near the fire. Applicants must be good swimmers, agile, and very fast. Pay: $150,000 per fire—plus funeral expenses if needed.

■ **WANTED:**
Mercenary Soldiers to fight guerrilla soldiers. Applicants must be proficient in use of firearms, skilled in ambush work, and understand the value of good life insurance. Pay: $500 a week and a $50,000 bonus for each year you stay alive.

■ **WANTED:**
Chemical Waste Disposal Workers to package, transport, and dispose of dangerous chemical waste. Applicants must be able to lift 50-pound barrels and carry their own cancer insurance. Pay: $1,000 a week plus all the toxic waste you'll ever need.

HAZARDOUS DUTY WARNING

Circle your group's assignment:

Paul (2 Corinthians 11:23-29)
Stephen (Acts 6:8-15; 7:54–8:3)

Read your assigned Scripture passage(s). Based on what you read, create a list of the risks associated with being a follower of Christ.

WARNING:

The Dangerous Duty Committee has determined that following Christ may be considered hazardous work. The risks associated with being a Christian include any or all of the following:

_____

_____

_____

_____

_____

_____

_____

_____

_____

_____

_____

_____

_____

Changed 4 Life

As your students go through these Bible studies, encourage them to begin keeping a journal. If you have enough money in your budget, buy a new spiral notebook for each student. Challenge teenagers to write in their journal for five minutes each day over a two-month period.

Explain that the topic of their journal will be "My Life as a Christian" and they'll have a chance to record their thoughts, questions, prayers, and ideas about what they'll learn each week during the four Bible studies in *Faith 4 Life: My Life as a Christian*. You'll help them out by providing journaling ideas for them. Simply photocopy page 47, give a copy to each student, and invite them to tape the questions inside their journal.

Give teenagers a weekly reminder to spend time writing each day. At the end of the two months, provide teenagers with an opportunity to publicly share with each other at least one way they've grown in their faith as a result of the Bible studies and daily journaling. Allow students to share excerpts from their journals if they would like to. (Be sure to respect the privacy of students who want to keep their journals completely private.) When teenagers are done sharing, spend some time praying for all of the students, asking God to strengthen them as they continue to grow in their daily lives as followers of Christ.

My Life as a Christian Journal Suggestions

Week 1: "Rock Solid Faith"
- How do I want to trust God more in my everyday life?
- What situations did I face this week that helped me grow in my trust in God?

Week 2: "Guided by God"
- How have I experienced the presence of the Holy Spirit in my life today?
- How can I listen more carefully to the Holy Spirit's guidance in my life?

Week 3: "Everyday Grace"
- Is it easy or hard for me to accept God's grace? Why?
- Why am I thankful for God's grace in my life? How does it affect me each day?

Week 4: "No Matter the Cost"
- When have I suffered because of my faith? Did it help me grow? Why or why not?
- Would I be willing to *really* suffer because of my faith in Christ? Would I be willing to die for it? Why or why not?

Week 5
- Do I know someone who has been a great example of trusting God? How has this person impacted my life?
- When I think about my life over the next year, how do I want to grow in my faith as a Christian?

Week 6
- When I look over the past few weeks, how have I grown in my relationship with the Holy Spirit?
- What is one specific situation or area in my life in which I need to rely on the Holy Spirit's guidance?

Week 7
- How have I grown in my understanding of God's grace in my life? How have I shared that grace with others?
- How would I describe my relationship with Jesus in just a few sentences?

Week 8
- How have other Christians been a good example to me when it comes to suffering for my faith in Christ?
- As I look back over everything I've written in this journal, how have I grown or changed in my understanding of what it means to be a Christian?

Look for the Whole Family of Faith 4 Life Bible Studies!

Coming Soon!

for Senior High
- Christian Character
- Following Jesus
- Worshipping 24/7
- Your Relationships

for Junior High
- Choosing Wisely
- How to Pray
- My Family Life
- Sharing Jesus

for Preteens
- Building Friendships
- Handling Conflict
- Succeeding in School
- What's a Christian?

Senior High Books
- Applying God's Word
- Believing in Jesus
- Family Matters
- Is There Life After High School?
- Prayer
- Sexuality
- Sharing Your Faith
- Your Christian ID

Junior High Books
- Becoming a Christian
- Fighting Temptation
- Finding Your Identity
- Friends
- God's Purpose for Me
- My Life as a Christian
- Understanding the Bible
- Who Is God?

Preteen Books
- Being Responsible
- Getting Along With Others
- God in My Life
- Going Through Tough Times
- How to Make Great Choices
- Peer Pressure
- The Bible and Me
- Why God Made Me

Visit your local Christian bookstore,
or contact Group Publishing, Inc., at 800-447-1070.
www.grouppublishing.com